The FIRST BOOK of
ARCHITECTURE

A City Square, *by Luciano da Laurana. (Courtesy of the Walters Art Gallery, Baltimore, Md.*

An artist's idea for a planned city consisting of a paved square surrounded by the kinds of buildings presented in this book: a memorial (triumphal arch), *center;* a stadium, *left;* a church (or chapel), *right;* and large buildings on either side for living, work, education, and the administration of public affairs.

The FIRST BOOK of
ARCHITECTURE

by Lamont Moore

Author of THE FIRST BOOK OF PAINTINGS

Franklin Watts, Inc. • 575 Lexington Avenue • New York 22

To my wife
HENRIETTA LANDELL MOORE
whose assistance and encouragement
helped to create it, this book is
dedicated

DESIGNED BY DAVID GOODNOUGH

Library of Congress Catalog Number: 61-5552
© Copyright 1961 by Lamont Moore
Printed in the United States of America
by Polygraphic Company of America, Inc.
FIRST PRINTING

CONTENTS

[CONTINUED ON NEXT PAGE]

INTRODUCTION

Architecture is the art of enclosing space for some human purpose. In ancient Greece the "master builder" supervised the construction of temples and other public buildings. From his title in Greek, *architekton*, comes our word, "architect."

Nowadays an architect must receive a great deal of scientific training in practical matters having to do with his profession. He must know mathematics, as well as many facts concerning materials — for example, what loads different materials may safely carry — so that there will be no danger of his buildings falling down.

Another part of an architect's education is concerned with the principles underlying beauty. We call these "aesthetic principles." They have to do with the elements that are shared by all the arts: line, shape, space, light, and color, controlled by pattern, balance, rhythm, contrast, and unity.

With these principles and with his scientific knowledge, the architect creates useful structures that give us pleasure, a sense of the beautiful. A fine building, then, is firmly constructed of good materials and serves its purpose well, while at the same time it gives us a feeling of beauty that is similar to the feelings we have when we hear music or enjoy painting and sculpture.

As we shall see in looking at some of the noted buildings of the past and present, architects are free to emphasize either of the two aspects of their art, sometimes the structural, sometimes the aesthetic, but most often they skillfully combine both aspects.

Let us look first at a renowned example of the art of architecture, the famous tomb known as the Taj Mahal.

The TAJ MAHAL stands near the town of Agra, India, at a bend in the Jumna River. It is a white marble tomb for Mumtaz Mahal, the beloved wife of Shah Jahan. He planned a similar structure for himself, to be built of black marble across the river, but he squandered so much money on his wife's memorial that he was not permitted even to start his own. He too is entombed in the Taj Mahal.

In brilliant sunlight or by the light of a full moon, the central dome seems to float in space. Four slender towers called minarets mark the corners of the great marble platform on which the building rests. They make the Taj appear larger than it really is. If you place a finger over

2

each pair of minarets in the picture, you will see that the building seems to shrink in size.

The domes swell out into space, but space flows into the deep arches arranged around the outside of the building. Over the central arch, even at a distance, you can see some of the elaborate patterns of leaves and flowers which decorate the building inside and out, sometimes carved, sometimes of inlay work in colored marbles and precious stones. The interior of the Taj is a shadowy, mysterious place containing the tombs, enclosed by a pierced marble screen.

Small domes differing slightly in shape from the large dome; straight and curving lines; exquisite decorations limited to certain spaces and leaving the rest of the walls clean and free to reflect the shifting lights and colors from the sky; shadowed porticoes into which the light reflects from the white platform: all these are elements that make the building a masterpiece of exterior design.

We do not know who planned the Taj Mahal. He created the setting for his gemlike building as carefully as he designed the building itself. He placed it to best advantage in a huge garden with a long, narrow reflecting pool in front and the river behind. Over the entrance gate, Arabic letters proclaim: "No one shall enter the garden of God unless he is pure in heart."

There have been many descriptions of the Taj Mahal and its enclosure. One French traveler admired the butterflies, squirrels, and beautiful parrots that were enjoying this earthly paradise, protected by guards in white muslin uniforms who were armed with peashooters to ward off crows and vultures. He wrote: "This place is both luminous and solemn . . . the poem in trees and flowers unites with the poem in marble to sing of splendor and peace."*

* Quoted from *In India, by* André Chevrillon, 1891.

Stonehenge.

ARCHITECTURE FOR WORSHIP

Architecture for worship has brought forth the best talents of architects in all times of history. They have used their scientific (engineering) skills to create new kinds of religious buildings. Frequently they have expressed the ennobling and uplifting spirit of religion in forms of unsurpassed beauty.

In visiting some of the best-known examples of architecture for worship, we begin by dropping down on Salisbury Plain in southern England to look at STONEHENGE, Place of the Hanging Stones. Four thousand years ago people who were still living in the Stone Age, using stone tools, raised this impressive structure.

4

It is not absolutely certain that this was a sacred place, but it seems reasonable to suppose that it must have been made for some form of worship, possibly directed toward the sun. In any event, Stonehenge was difficult to construct and would be so even today, with modern tools and machines.

Huge stones were shaped, perhaps by splitting with the help of fire and cold water, then moved on rolling logs to their present location. Here they were set up according to a definite plan.

How was this done? The unknown builders of Stonehenge were very capable engineers. Using picks made of deer horns, they scraped ramps in the soft chalk ground. The stone posts were tilted up until they slid down the slopes into holes at the bottom, to stand vertically. Other huge stones, the lintels, were raised by means of ropes from scaffolds and were placed horizontally on top of the stone posts — their ends interlocked.

The ground plan at the left shows the arrangement of posts and lintels as well as the rings of standing stones without lintels. There may have been a roof of logs, covered with straw to shed water.

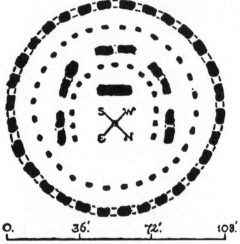

0.   36.   72.   108.

From Stonehenge Today and Yesterday, *by Frank Stevens. (Reproduced by permission of the Controller of Her Britannic Majesty's Stationery Office)*

Other circles of stones arranged by men have been found in England, but Stonehenge is the one worked out in the most detail. It has endured as a grand and mysterious example of architecture in its beginnings, achieved with the "post and lintel" construction still in use today.

5

The SHODEN is one of three buildings that form the Ise Shrine in Japan, a most sacred place for followers of the Shinto religion. They believe that here the "Mirror of Justice," given to them by the Sun-Goddess, is preserved forever in the very spot that she chose.

The Shoden and its companion storehouses represent a very ancient form of Japanese architecture. The original wooden structures have not lasted through the centuries, but in a sense they have defied time because every twenty years new buildings exactly like the old are erected on a neighboring location. Then the old buildings are torn down to make room for the new copies twenty years later. All this building up and tearing down began about 675 A.D.

There is no mistaking that this structure is a treasure house. No doors or windows can be seen. Sheltering the entire ground space occupied by the building is a great roof, thatched with shredded bark and held down by short lengths of heavy logs, which keep the wind from blowing it away. As in most Oriental architecture, the roof is a very important feature.

The large post standing free from the end wall supports the ridge-pole, on which the rafters rest. (One rafter at each end is very long and juts skyward.) The end post is made larger than necessary so that when we look at it we shall be impressed with its size and so shall be convinced that it *is* strong.

Slender posts support a veranda with a delicate railing. This light, floating appearance at the base of a structure comes about because the Japanese prefer to leave uncovered the framing and supporting parts of their buildings. They wish to see the skeleton. This Oriental point of view has been adopted in recent years by Western architects, who have learned much from the architecture of Japan.

6

The Shoden, Ise Shrine, Japan. (Courtesy of the Kokusai Bunka Shinkokai, Tokyo)

Hall of Columns, Temple of Karnak, Egypt.

8

The ancient Egyptians used stone as their principal building material. Stone is brittle and heavy. The columns of the Temple of Karnak therefore crowd close together — so close, in fact, that they take up most of the space in the famous HALL OF COLUMNS. The tops of the columns are carved to resemble the flowers of papyrus and lotus plants, which grew along the river Nile. More than one hundred columns were needed to support beams, which carried the stone slabs forming the roof.

Sculptured figures of gods and kings, some of them twenty feet high, decorate the sides of the columns. Originally, as the model below shows us, they were brilliantly painted.

A worshiper in an Egyptian temple went from large to small spaces and from light to dark. He could not enter the innermost room, just as in Japan no one but the emperor and a priest could enter the Shoden. When the Hall of Columns had its roof, it must have been a welcome relief from the hot sun of the courtyard.

The architect made provision for air and light to enter the hall by erecting higher columns in the central part. Just below the lintels of the roof, he placed pierced stone windows. Although it is now roofless and in ruins, the hall is a masterpiece of ancient Egyptian building — an immense, awe-inspiring example of religious architecture.

Model of Hall of Columns, Temple of Karnak. (Courtesy of the Metropolitan Museum of Art, New York — Bequest of Levi Hale Willard, 1883)

The PARTHENON stands in ruined majesty atop the hill of the Acropolis in Athens, Greece. The location is one of the most splendid in the world. This temple which honored Athena Parthenos, patron goddess of the city, was built in the fifth century B.C. As with the Shoden in Japan, people could approach the building and take part in religious processions around it. Only a few, however, could enter the two small rooms inside, one a treasury and the other the Chamber of the Goddess. Her statue, carved in gold and ivory, occupied most of the space in the narrow hall.

The space of the Parthenon is on the outside. It flows into the walkway around the building, formed by the columns which once supported a roof having two triangular ends called "pediments." Like the Taj Mahal, the building rests on a high platform which sets it apart from its surroundings and gives it a firm base.

10

Model of the Parthenon. (Courtesy of the Metropolitan Museum of Art, New York — Bequest of Levi Hale Willard, 1883.) See interior view below, showing reconstructed statue of Athena.

The Parthenon is a supreme example of post and lintel construction. It is essentially a large piece of sculpture created in Grecian marble, one of the finest materials either for shaping rounded forms or squaring off to knifelike edges.

The columns were made of "drums" carefully fitted one on top of another without mortar to bind them together, then channeled with "flutings" to lighten their appearance. They seem to be straight-sided and elegant when viewed from a distance, even though their sides are slightly curved.

The model pictured above shows the building as it may have appeared. The pediments contained carved and painted figures of the goddess, other gods, and superhuman beings. Sculptures lower down represented human beings, notably a long procession with horses and riders coming to pay homage to the gods. Most of these masterpieces of sculpture have been removed to museums for safekeeping.

The Parthenon was an outstanding civic building as well as a place of worship. It represented the power of Athens when it was built. It is now a monument to the precision, refinement, clarity, and strength of ancient Greek art and thought.

Doric

Ionic

Tuscan

CAPITALS OF CLASSIC ORDERS

Corinthian

Composite

Pillars and columns often dignify large public buildings and sometimes even private homes. The tops of the columns are called "capitals." They were first designed by the Greeks and have been used down through the ages with certain changes made principally by the Romans. Check back to see what kinds of capitals were used in the Parthenon. You will find that they are the plainest: the Doric type, or "order." In determining each order, the capital, shaft, and base of the column are all considered.

The Greeks used columns to bear weight, to work for the buildings of which they were parts. When the Romans perfected the arched construction described on the opposite page, they often used columns and half columns not as working parts, but as decorations.

When you pass a building with columns, look at the capitals to see which of the above classic designs have been used.

Roman aqueduct bridge, Nimes, France. (Photo, John B. Bayley.) Water flowed in trough at top to city from mountain streams.

The Arch

Up to this point we have considered only post and lintel construction. We now look at another form known as "vaulted construction." It was made possible by the arch. Although the Egyptians and Greeks knew how to build them, arches were not used extensively until the Romans developed them to solve many architectural problems.

The arch is an arrangement of wedge-shaped blocks which, when fitted together over an opening, can carry a load by wedging themselves into balance. The ends of the arch thrust outward to the side. This thrust is held in check by heavy, vertical masses called "abutments." If arches are built one behind another, the result is a long room with a curved ceiling called a "barrel vault." If abutments with half arches are built in a circle, one right next to another, the result is a circular room with a ceiling called a "dome."

Vaulted construction produced huge buildings made up of small units such as bricks or cut stone. The Romans often combined these with concrete for massive inside walls faced with brick or marble. The resulting structures were stupendous feats both of engineering and architectural design.

The Pantheon.

Model of the Pantheon. (Courtesy of the Metropolitan Museum of Art, New York — Bequest of Levi Hale Willard, 1883)

The PANTHEON is the only building of Imperial Rome to have withstood successfully the ravages of time and man. The porch reminds us of the Parthenon, but one can clearly see that the columns are Corinthian rather than Doric. The lettering over the porch indicates that the building was begun by Marcus Agrippa. It was completed about 120 A.D., during the reign of the Emperor Hadrian.

Stepping past the original bronze doors, we move back into history and enjoy one of the most harmoniously proportioned interiors in the world. Proportion is the relation of all the parts to the whole. If a column appears too short or too tall, we say that it is "in bad proportion" to the rest of the building.

The dome of the Pantheon, constructed of concrete, is 142 feet across and rests on a collar of masonry 20 feet thick, which is faced with colored marbles. Light enters through a ceiling window, the "eye," which is 30 feet across and 140 feet from the marble pavement inlaid in patterns.

14

The interior of the Pantheon, a painting by Giovanni Panini. (Courtesy of the National Gallery of Art, Washington, D.C. — Samuel H. Kress Collection)

The picture on this page was painted in the late 1700's, after the Pantheon had been converted into a Christian church. It shows the light cast on the wall and illuminating the Corinthian capitals of the fluted columns carved from precious yellow marble. We also see elegant ladies, some at prayer, others conversing. Gentlemen look up in admiration at the dome.

Each visitor feels free to walk in any direction because of the circular shape of the great room. The round plan was very suitable for a temple originally dedicated to all the Roman gods: it did not favor any one deity. The people pictured here are experiencing the noble, motionless, and golden-colored space of the Pantheon, as many have before them and many since.

15

Interior of Hagia Sophia after it had been adapted for a Turkish mosque. The four minarets outside the building were erected then (see opposite page).

After the Roman Empire was overthrown, the city of Constantinople (now Istanbul) became the center of the civilized world. One of the great rulers was Justinian who commissioned the architect, Anthemius of Tralles, to design a large church for the city.

Anthemius knew a great deal about geometry. His church, HAGIA SOPHIA, is a combination of rectangles, circles and squares, cubes, and spheres cut in half to make domes and cut again to make half domes. The arrangement of these forms and the space contained by them is one of the architectural masterpieces of the entire world.

The innermost space is covered by two half domes and the vast central dome, which seems to float overhead. You will recall that the dome of the Pantheon rests on a collar the same size as the rim. The dome of Hagia Sophia rests on four enormous arches, which form a square. The triangular spaces in the corners are filled with supports called "pendentives," because they appear to be hanging (pendent) from the dome.

Pendentives were not used by the Romans. They were invented by Eastern architects and represent another step in the history of construction.

Look at the drawing representing the church cut through the middle. You will see that the central portion is a single space from floor to roof. This is surrounded by an outer shell, which is two stories high and composed of small rooms. The building thereby contains the element of contrast, important in all the arts. We

(Reproduced from Hagia Sophia, *by E. H. Swift, Columbia University Press, 1940, with permission of author and publisher)*

move first into small spaces and then into one huge space. Like Alice in Wonderland, we feel taller and uplifted.

During the morning hours, the light streams in through the high windows to illumine the altar at the far end. In the Pantheon, the visitor does not feel compelled to move in any particular direction. Here he is led forward by a glimpse of the half-domed space beyond. The church is thus planned around its center and, at the same time, it entices visitors to walk its length.

The architect took pains to control the feeling of almost limitless space by banding the walls with two heavy, projecting cornices. They appear to be holding in the walls sheathed to the upper cornice with colored marbles. Above, glittering mosaics of gold and colored glass create mysterious pictures shining down from the heights. Once these were covered with whitewash, but now they are being carefully uncovered.

Today the church is a museum. Eventually it will appear approximately as it did in the sixth century A.D., a masterpiece of architectural planning which inspired churches in Italy and Greece, mosques in the Near East, and synagogues bordering the Mediterranean Sea.

18

Notre Dame.

A flight from Istanbul to Paris leaves Hagia Sophia behind and brings us to architecture of the Middle Ages in France, five hundred years later.

Let us imagine that we are walking toward NOTRE DAME, the Cathedral of Paris. We notice that the façade (the front of the building) is horizontally divided into sections. There are three stone doorways at ground level. Their pointed arches are decorated with sculptured stone figures.

The Kings of Judah stand above the portals, each in his own niche. They form a band all the way across the façade. Above them, in the center, an enormous round window called a "rose window" is framed in stonework suggesting the petals of an open rose.

Slender columns and arches form the next horizontal section, and crowning all are two lordly towers. It is possible to climb up inside the towers and come out on the balcony to examine the gargoyles. Gargoyles are usually projecting waterspouts, carved in the strange shapes of mythical monsters. When the cathedral was refurbished in the 1800's, the architect in charge created seated gargoyles which gaze somberly from their parapets.

Notre Dame is one of the best-known churches in the world. It stands on an island in the Seine River where the city of Paris began. Notre

Notre Dame: gargoyles (above); interior (on opposite page).

Dame was started during the Middle Ages, about the year 1000 A.D., when many other large churches were being constructed throughout France.

By this time in history, great advances had been made in both engineering and tools. Architects formerly had designed churches with stone ceilings supported by round arches like Roman arches. These arched ceilings, or vaults, were heavy. Thick walls had to be built to support the thrust of the weight of the vaults.

Now came a new method of ceiling construction. Ribs of stone, light in weight and slightly pointed in shape, carried the weight of the stone slabs of the vault and channeled the weight down to the thin columns, which rested on heavy columns, as you can see in the picture on the next page.

Since the walls were free from bearing the weight of the vaults, they were no longer necessary for support. Walls became windows, filled with glass stained in brilliant colors. The pieces of glass, arranged to form pictures from Bible stories, threw patterns of colored light on columns and floor.

Around the end of the church — the "apse" — the vaulting was very complicated. In order to keep the walls free and to carry the weight outside, the builders made bridges of stone to connect the vaults to pillars, or "piers," which stand away from the building. These bridges and piers are know as "flying buttresses" because they seem to be springing from the ground up into the air.

The tall, thin spire, pointing like a finger to heaven, is called a "flèche," the French word for arrow. It also was made in the 1800's to replace a previous spire, which had become shaky with age.

Cathedrals of medieval times are supreme examples of architecture for worship. The lofty, narrow interior space makes us raise our eyes toward heaven and lifts our spirit. These great structures are memorials to the hundreds of workers whose names are not recorded, but who worked for the glory of God with daring, humility, patience, and love.

22

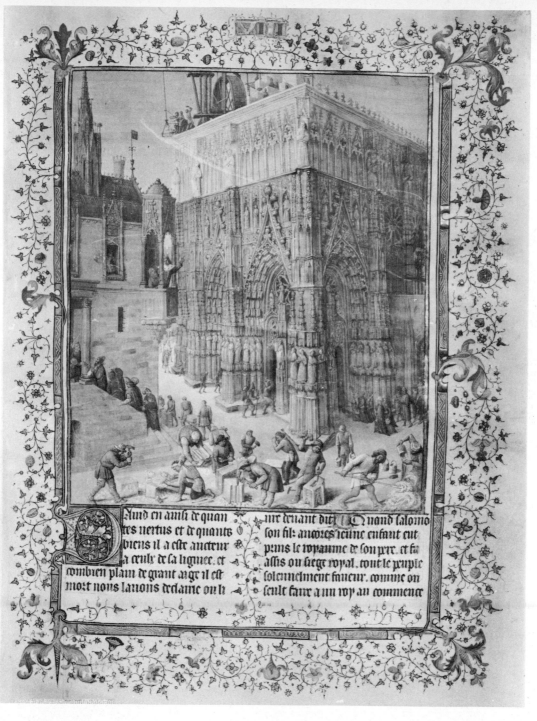

Page from a book of the Middle Ages now in the National Library, Paris. The illustration, painted by J. Fouquet, shows the building of a church, with workmen in the foreground, a king, and possibly the master builder in the balcony of the building on the left.

St. Peter's Basilica.

Toward the end of the Middle Ages, a different type of architecture appeared in Italy, where architects had become interested in ancient Roman buildings and took many ideas from them. The Pantheon, for example, was a great source of inspiration, as were the ruins of other ancient structures.

This interest in the past was only a part of a trend toward studying all phases of ancient civilizations. "Renaissance" is a French word meaning "rebirth" and it is used to describe this great period of study and activity between the Middle Ages and modern times.

The most famous Renaissance church and the largest Christian church in the world is St. Peter's Basilica, in Rome. It is called a "basilica"

Cardinal Polignac Visiting St. Peter's, Rome, by Giovanni Panini. (Courtesy of the Metropolitan Museum of Art, New York — Purchase, 1871)

because the plan of the building is similar to the older St. Peter's, built on the same location by early Christians. Because they did not want to copy pagan Roman temples, they followed the plan of a Roman basilica, a building used for business rather than worship. The plan consists of a broad central aisle, called the "nave," and two narrow side aisles — a plan also used in the churches of the Middle Ages, such as Notre Dame in Paris.

The Renaissance architects who designed the new St. Peter's built a wide nave, similar to that of the old church, and roofed it with a gorgeous, gilded and painted, Roman-style barrel vault. Corinthian flat columns were sunk into marble walls and were so covered with sculptured and painted details that it is quite difficult to see that the columns are supposed to support a long lintel with a rich cornice, jutting just below the arching vault. Toward the apse, the vault is broken by a vast circular space. Michelangelo, the famous architect-artist, designed the enormous dome that creates this space.

Approach to St. Peter's.

The dome attracts our eyes from a great distance. Its sides are more
steeply sloped than those of the dome of the Pantheon. Many architects
after Michelangelo used the dome of St. Peter's as a model.

The impressive approach to the Basilica is an important part of the
over-all plan. It was laid out by other architects, one of whom, Bernini,
created the famous "colonnades." These are two curving arms formed

26

by huge columns, which frame the space and draw us toward the entrance to the church.

A square, directly in front of the church, connects with the huge oval in the foreground. The pavement, patterned with white lines of light-colored stone, forms a floor for this enormous outdoor room furnished with two tall fountains and, in the center, a pointed pillar called an "obelisk."

The obelisk is Egyptian. Brought to ancient Rome by the Emperor Caligula, it was moved to its present position in 1586 under the supervision of the architect Fontana. His task was difficult — to move, without breaking, this huge piece of stone weighing over three hundred tons. The story of the raising of the obelisk to an upright position after it had been moved is one of those well-known in engineering and architectural history.

As the critical moment approached to set the stone in place, the great crowd of workmen employed in the project were commanded to work silently. In fact, the death penalty threatened anyone who spoke. While the obelisk was momentarily poised, all the ropes that supported it strained to the breaking point, one of the workmen cried out. He realized that the dry ropes would hold if they were wet. Quickly he shouted, "Water on the ropes." Water was brought and the task was successfully completed.

Instead of being killed for having spoken, the workman — with his descendants — was given the honor of supplying the palms for St. Peter's on Palm Sunday.

The dome and the obelisk! Both point to the arching sky that forms the curved ceiling for this square, one of the three most noted squares in the world, the setting for St. Peter's, one of the most imposing examples of architecture for worship.

Tribute to Sir Christopher Wren, a fanciful drawing by Charles R. Cockerell (1836), showing all of Wren's buildings in England.

In 1666 the Great Fire of London destroyed a section known as "The City," including fifty churches and St. Paul's Cathedral. A famous architect, Christopher Wren, rebuilt the cathedral and many of the churches. In the picture you can see the great dome of the new St. Paul's overshadowing everything else and reminding us of St. Peter's.

It took many years to complete the cathedral. The building of the smaller churches progressed more speedily. Small-sized lots gave the architect many problems. He was clever at solving them, for he designed each building with as much space as possible inside. Everyone could see and hear the minister. Wren's churches, therefore, resembled auditoriums.

The exterior of the building was plain except for the steeple, which could be seen from afar. All of Wren's steeples are different. He took ideas from the Italian Renaissance and built up spires with layer upon layer of columns, arches, railings, and urns, capping them sometimes with small domes and slender obelisks.

Many architects have followed patterns set by Christopher Wren. To the plain exterior of a Wren church, one of his followers, James Gibbs, often added a Roman-style temple front with columns and pediment.

St. Michael's, in Charleston, South Carolina, (built 1752-1761) is a fine example of this popular design, used all over America even in modern times.

In New England such churches are usually built of wood and painted white. In the South, brick and wood are combined and sometimes, as in St. Michael's, the brickwork is coated with stucco, a kind of rough plaster.

St. Michael's.

Wayne Andrews

In our examples of architecture for worship we have seen many churches that are enormous, with ample floor space for people to stand upon, be seated, or kneel in prayer. Above them, domes or vaults enclose vast space, mysterious, eternal, a wonder to experience. We now end this section of the book with a visit to a chapel, or small church, at Ronchamp, France, built on the side of a hill, close to the sky.

When was it built? Who was the architect? The chapel, like the Parthenon in Greece, commands the site on which it stands. Air and light flow into it, but not through columns, as they do in the Greek temple. The roof is thick and dark and sheltering and it could protect a sacred object as the roof of the Shoden does in faraway Japan.

The architect was neither Greek nor Japanese. He was born in Switzerland, but spent most of his life in France, where he took the name, Le Corbusier. As a young man, he started out to be an artist. He made friends with other artists who were establishing the art of the twentieth century. They were creating new and different designs, using very simple forms: circles, cylinders, squares, rectangles, and straight lines.

During a trip to Greece, Le Corbusier spent six weeks studying the Parthenon and was so inspired by it that, on his return to Paris, he decided to become an architect. He learned how to construct buildings of concrete reinforced with metal rods. He experimented with this material throughout his career of building houses, apartments, and even an entire city in India, Chandigarh.

The CHAPEL OF NOTRE DAME at Ronchamp was built from 1950 to 1955. You can see that the structure is quite different from post and lintel or arch and vault construction. The walls seem to be molded. They curve and lean inward, inviting us to enter. The roof on one side protects an outdoor altar and pulpit. On the other side you can see a tower, which has a large window in it to let light into the chapel. There are other such towers, which are hidden by the roof in the picture.

30

Chapel of Notre Dame, Ronchamp.

[NOTE: It would be interesting to look for pictures of other buildings by Le Corbusier, to see the great variety of his work. Sometimes he supported his structures on strong posts, which permit air and light to flow underneath. Sometimes his roofs are gardens and sundecks. He made walls of glass. He experimented with lighting, soundproofing, and air conditioning, and in various ways pioneered in many things now considered important in architecture.]

The interior of the chapel at Ronchamp is a "place of silence, of prayer, of peace, of spiritual joy," to use the architect's own words. The wall at the left slopes outward, the reverse of its inward sloping on the exterior. Many windows of different sizes pierce the thick wall. In each one a few panes of glass, painted by the architect with designs, admit a joyful light into the hushed, austere room.

The shape of the roof was inspired by a crab's shell that Le Corbusier picked up on the shore of Long Island, N.Y. The roof is made of two thin skins of concrete. It does not rest on the walls, but on small posts that rise above them. As a result, the roof seems to float, a canopy resting on a thin crack of light, as the architect said, "to amaze" us.

Yes, a chapel can be small in size and yet impress us as much as a great cathedral. Architecture for worship, finely built, useful for its purpose, pleasing to look at and move about in, its spaces, masses, and lines understandable to us, is architecture in one of its highest forms.

ARCHITECTURE FOR LIVING

Men have built many kinds of homes, depending on different climates and the different building materials at hand. For example, in southwestern United States, where lumber is scarce and the climate very dry, the Indians mixed earth and water, which they shaped into large bricks and baked in the sun. This building material, called "adobe," is excellent for keeping out summer heat and winter cold. It was, therefore, good to use for building pueblos.

Below is a picture of TAOS PUEBLO, New Mexico. (Pueblo is the Spanish word for "town.") You can see how the individual flat-roofed houses form, together, one large building like an apartment house.

It is obvious that the pueblo was not planned by an architect. It just grew, as families needed space. Even so, the entire structure is as majestic as the mountains behind it, and its clear arrangement of simple, solid shapes almost gives us the impression that one man built it.

Originally there were very few doors in the pueblo. The owners climbed ladders and entered through the roofs of their homes. This plan was necessary in case of enemy attack, for then the ladders were hauled up and the town became a fortress similar to the medieval castle that we shall consider on the next page.

Taos Pueblo.

Bodiam Castle.

Architects who designed castles had to keep many things in mind, because a castle served many purposes. It was a fortress, a home, a factory. There was a room set aside for worship — the chapel — as well as a Great Hall, a place for business meetings and entertainment. Life in the castle must have been very busy when everything needed for carrying it on was prepared or manufactured entirely inside the castle walls.

BODIAM CASTLE, England, was built about 1386, toward the end of the Middle Ages. It is therefore a "young castle" and very well preserved. Many other castles were destroyed by wars, or allowed to fall into ruins when people left them to live in cities.

The castle was, first of all, a fortress. It was like an island. A moat of water surrounded the high, thick walls. On top of the walls there were walkways where men could stand at notches, to shoot out arrows and other missiles. The flat walls could be guarded from round towers at each corner of the building.

Notice that the square tower, the rear entrance to the castle, differs at the top from the round towers. Small arches project from the square tower's wall, and under each arch is a hole leading to the tower platform or roof. Men on the platform could pour boiling oil and drop iron balls down through these holes.

Sometimes the enemy succeeded in climbing the walls, but even if he reached the inner courtyard, he had difficulty in capturing the inhabitants. They were quite well protected by the arrangement of rooms and could hold out, defending the few doorways.

The plan of the castle developed from its need to be an efficient machine against invasion. It could also be arranged for reasonably pleasant living in peaceful days. Oftentimes colored tapestries decorated the walls of the living quarters. Bright fires and torches warmed and lighted the Great Hall on winter evenings. Like the Indian pueblo, also a defensive building, the castle impresses us with its massive shape and strong outline against the sky.

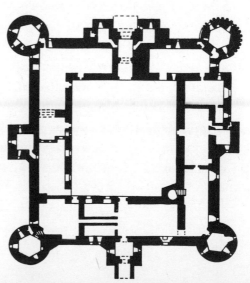

Bodiam Castle Plan. (Reproduced from *Architecture in Britain*, by G. Webb, Penguin Books, Ltd., with permission of author and publisher)

PAUL REVERE's HOUSE in Boston, Massachusetts, is an example of the kind of home built in New England by the early settlers. It has a steep roof to carry off rains and melting snow. The second floor projects slightly out over the sidewalk. The windows are very small, made of diamond-shaped panes set in lead strips, because glass was expensive.

The stout door leads to the hall and an enclosed stairway. This was a practical arrangement making it possible to go directly upstairs without having to pass through ground-floor rooms. The façade is therefore unbalanced, with the door on the right instead of in the center.

If you go to England, you will find houses similar to Paul Revere's and you will be surprised to learn that they were made in the very late Middle Ages. Steep roofs, sidewalk overhangs, leaded windows, shutters, sturdy doors — all these features are medieval, repeated in this house of the 1600's when medieval days had passed for more than a century.

What we call "domestic architecture," the architecture of homes, always seems to lag behind the architecture of churches and public build-

36

ings. Even in the United States today, there are not as many "modern" homes as there are banks and service stations and supermarkets designed along new lines.

In England, where winters are mild, the builders often omitted the long, horizontal clapboards that overlap each other on the outside of Paul Revere's house. A cage of stout timbers filled in with brick or plaster, with the timbers left uncovered, is the usual construction for the English "half-timbered" house.* Practical reasons kept the low-ceilinged rooms small, so that they could be heated effectively by fireplaces.

Paul Revere's house was also a workshop. We usually think of Revere as a messenger, riding his white horse through the night to warn of the British attack. We should also remember him as a master craftsman who employed several helpers in a small factory that was part of his house. Here he created beautiful pieces of silverware which are now treasured heirlooms and prized museum pieces.

* Look for pictures of such houses in illustrated articles on England. Anne Hathaway's cottage is a noted example.

Interior, Paul Revere's House.

Plan: House of the Golden Wedding.

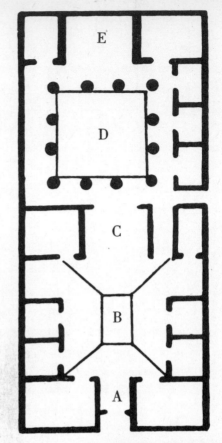

In the year 79 A.D., Mount Vesuvius, in Italy, erupted violently and buried the town of Pompeii under tons of lightweight volcanic stone. Most of the inhabitants fled the city, but a few were caught. Centuries later, archaeologists found them under the powdery, suffocating stone.

The archaeologists also discovered that the houses, shops, and public buildings were miraculously preserved. We therefore know a great deal about house architecture of the Roman Empire.

If you walk down the paved street and enter the HOUSE OF THE SILVER WEDDING* by the hall (A on plan), you will view the interior as it appears in the photograph on the opposite page. You look up to the sky through the roof window of the atrium (B) or directly ahead to the tablinum (C) and the columned peristyle (D) that encloses the garden.

The atrium contained a rectangular pool to catch rain water from the roof. Doorways led to sleeping rooms and storerooms. The tablinum was used as a library or office. To the left was the triclinium or dining room. The peristyle's columns supported tile roofs that sheltered other sleeping rooms, the kitchen, and the exedra (E), a secluded, private space at the back of the house.

* So named because its uncovering was completed in 1893 in the presence of the King and Queen of Italy, then celebrating their twenty-fifth wedding anniversary.

The plan of a Roman house was orderly, convenient, and easy to move through. There was a pleasant changing back and forth of light and shadow. The cool, softly lighted atrium contrasted with the bright street and the sunshine-filled peristyle. The private rooms were quite dark. Many modern houses suggest a similar arrangement of space, with one room opening into another.

The Medici were one of the most noted families in Italy. They lived in the city of Florence at the beginning of the Renaissance period. Michelozzo, who was a Florentine architect, was commissioned to build a palace for them.

In previous times impressive castle dwellings had been built by rulers of noble birth. The Medici were bankers and businessmen, however. They ruled the city-state of Florence not as kings, but as citizens. Their encouragement of learning and the arts helped advance civilization. Since their time, wealthy people have frequently lived in large homes and, like the Medici family, have used their wealth to benefit mankind in various ways.

As you can see, the MEDICI PALACE stands at a busy corner of the city. Michelozzo used architectural features from buildings of the Middle Ages as well as those of ancient Rome. The walls on the ground floor are built of rough stone. Originally there were no large windows at ground level — only doorways and smaller windows. Above the rough stone is a band of smoother stonework and, at the top, a heavy cornice inspired by the architecture of Roman buildings. The pairs of windows on the second and third floors, however, are like those in buildings of medieval times.

A stone shield carved with the Medici coat of arms is attached to the corner of the palace. This "sign" with seven balls was another relic of the age of chivalry, when knights bore identifying devices painted on their shields.

The arms also decorate the beautiful inside courtyard, which gives light and air to the rooms above. A short hall connects with the street through the great door, which could be shut against intruders to make the palace a stronghold.

On opposite page: Medici Palace.

Photo by Alinari, Florence

Alinari, Florence

Courtyard, Medici Palace.

Compare the windows of the second floor with those in the upper picture on the opposite page. They are very much alike. The little painting (page 43) was finished just about the time the Medici palace was built. Two cranes lift materials from the ground. Bricks baked in ovens at the right are being used for the upper part of the tower.

Also compare the windows of the imaginary palace in the lower picture on the opposite page with the first-floor, exterior windows of the Medici palace. (See preceding page.) Such windows, topped with pointed pediments, became popular in Renaissance buildings.

The Building of the Tower of Babel, by an unknown Flemish artist (about 1480). (Reproduced through the courtesy of the Johan Maurits van Nassau Foundation, Mauritshuis, The Hague, Netherlands)

BELOW: *The Building of a Palace,* by an unknown Florentine artist (about 1480). (From the John and Mabel Ringling Museum of Art, Sarasota, Florida)

Monticello.

We now look at a small palace of the American Renaissance, the home of Thomas Jefferson, third President of the United States. It is located on top of "Little Mountain," near Charlottesville, Virginia, and is visited by thousands of Americans every year.

Jefferson was a man of many talents. He was an inventor and a gifted amateur architect. He designed and supervised the construction of his house and called it MONTICELLO, the Italian word for "little mountain." He also conceived the basic design for the Capitol in Washington, D.C., which we shall visit later.

At Monticello there are many classical features, combined with new

Entrance hall, Monticello.

and original ideas. Two porches, in the manner of Roman temples with Tuscan columns, form the entrances at each end of a central hall. A shallow dome crowns the upper part of the structure, which is also decorated with railings.

Jefferson began building at Monticello in 1768, making bricks in a kiln on the property. For the next forty years he enjoyed watching his home grow, and designed the gardens and landscaping so that the house and its setting would make a complete whole.

One of the features of Monticello is the variety of windows. Round and fan-shaped windows light the upper floors. The high-ceilinged ground-floor rooms have very tall sash windows to admit as much air as possible in the summertime. Sash windows slide up and down, unlike the casement windows in Paul Revere's house, which open from the sides.

The first floor contains the living and dining rooms, master bedroom, library, and study. Narrow, hidden stairs lead to guest rooms and the ballroom under the dome, and connect with the basement kitchen, workshop, and stables. One of Jefferson's numerous gadgets and inventions is the cannon-ball calendar clock over the front door. As the cannon-ball weights fall, they pass marks on the wall that indicate the days of the week.

45

Place Vendôme.

We have been looking at houses planned for individual families. As cities grew, buildings were needed in which several families could live. Architects became involved with over-all plans for cities that included streets, parks, offices, and stores as well as houses.

The city of Paris is famous for its plan consisting of parks, broad avenues, and squares with buildings grouped around them. The PLACE VENDÔME is one of the most beautiful squares in the world. Houses of uniform height enclose the space on eight sides to form an octagon. The ground floors of each house contain shops, and above these are spacious apartments. Napoleon's column, inspired by that of the Emperor Trajan in Rome, rises proudly in the center.

Plans for Parisian squares like the Place Vendôme, built for the wealthy, were adapted in later times for the dwellings of people with moderate incomes.

In the twentieth century, northern European countries led the way toward improving the housing for large numbers of office and factory workers. MERCATOR SQUARE, on the outskirts of Amsterdam, is an example of this kind of plan. Each block of buildings has its own inner court. This arrangement provides light and air for every apartment. Public transportation from the square takes people into the city. The country is just a few steps away. Perhaps someday, through further advances in architecture for living, all the peoples of the world will be healthfully housed in pleasant surroundings.

Mercator Square.

KLM Photo (Courtesy Netherlands Information Service)

Brick factory building.

ARCHITECTURE FOR EARNING

Architecture for earning is one of the most important types of architecture developed in the United States. At first, factories were in homes. Paul Revere and his assistants made silverware in his house. When he was asked to make the copper plates for the dome of the State House, in Boston, he had to find larger quarters.

As manufacturing increased, factories were built of brick with fancy towers and windows. Gradually these unnecessary decorations disappeared. Businessmen needed larger buildings, and architects learned to span enormous spaces with metal beams supported by a few metal or concrete columns reinforced with metal rods.

Albert Kahn was one of the most successful industrial architects. He planned several of the huge structures required for the assembly of automobiles. While his buildings are strictly for use and not beauty, their horizontal lines, bands of windows, and roof design create a kind of majestic architecture.

DeSoto Plant, by Kahn.

Prudential Building.

Louis Sullivan was the "father" of modern architecture in the United States. He designed buildings with new ideas that have shaped American architecture since his time. He disapproved of classical stone columns and sculpture because they disguised buildings that were beginning to be constructed essentially of metal.

Up until eighty years ago, the height of a building was limited by the amount of weight the walls could carry. High buildings required very thick masonry walls, which took up valuable inside floor space.

New methods, devised at the end of the 1890's, made use of metal beams and columns encased in masonry or concrete. The beam supported only the single story that rested upon it, and therefore the wall could be very thin. The weight passed to the ends of each beam and was carried downward by the vertical columns to which the beams were attached. This method made higher buildings possible.

The PRUDENTIAL BUILDING, Buffalo, New York, was designed by Sullivan. The lines of the first two stories are strongly horizontal, suggesting a firm foundation for the building that rises ten stories. The windows are divided by slender, continuous bands that suggest columns supporting the floors. Flat ornamentation, invented by the architect, enriches but does not hide the structure. This is not the first building of its kind, but from such construction the skyscraper was born.

Radio City.

Thomas Airviews

The invention of safe elevators was as important as new methods of construction in making possible skyscraper cities like RADIO CITY in New York. Actually this arrangement of buildings — as its proper name, Rockefeller Center, indicates — is not a city in itself, but a center. In fact, it serves as a civic center for the largest city of the Western Hemisphere.

Each day thousands of people come here to work or be entertained, to shop, or just to stroll. They can enter the buildings underground as well as from the street. High-speed elevators whisk them where they want to go.

Each floor is built so that daylight has to travel only 27 feet from the windows to the innermost space, next to the central core of elevator shafts. The buildings are therefore very thin, made up of steel frames, concrete, and stone in narrow slabs. Some sections do not run all the way up, but stop and form platforms on which grass and flowers are planted to create gardens in the sky. You can see two of these on the lowest buildings, in the foreground of the picture.

In contrast, the RCA Building, housing radio and television studios as well as offices, rises seventy stories — seven times higher than Louis Sullivan's building, which was constructed by essentially the same methods. Unlike Sullivan's Prudential Building, the RCA Building's horizontal lines are slighted in favor of soaring verticals, and the structure, like its neighbors, rushes up without even stopping. There is no cornice at the top to say, "This is the end!"

A walk between the two lower buildings in the picture and then down the steps to the terrace, is an unforgettable experience. We have the impression of standing at the bottom of a well and looking up, up, up. We are filled with awe that man, the architect and engineer, could have achieved such a splendid conquering of space.

Most of Rockefeller Center was completed in 1939, the MANUFACTURERS TRUST BUILDING in 1954. You can readily see a difference in construction. Glass has become very important — a special kind of glass formed of two sheets with an airless space between, to act as an insulator against heat and cold.

Storekeepers have long known the value of attractive window displays. In colonial days, "bow front" windows curved out over sidewalks. Windows became larger and larger. The Manufacturers Trust Building can be called showcase architecture, not to sell goods, but to sell banking services.

The interior is so beautifully arranged that people, as they pass, linger to look in. Often they enter because it is so inviting. The chief attraction is a huge safe, clearly visible from the street.

Louis Sullivan would have admired the balance of horizontals and verticals as well as the "shadow" cornice capped by the railing of the roof garden.

Manufacturers Trust Building.

Wayne Andrews

Architecture for travelers has always been an important section of architecture for earning. Air travel created the air terminal, a large project made up of land and buildings for various purposes. The NEW YORK INTERNATIONAL AIRPORT at Idlewild is now the eastern gateway to our country. At night its beacon flashes a welcome, just as the Statue of Liberty's torch greeted travelers in days when most people arrived by boat.

The architects, mindful that visitors from overseas should receive a good first impression of our country, have achieved a splendid arrangement of landscape and architecture. The Fountain of Liberty throws its waters high into the air. Other fountains and reflecting pools catch the light. Walkways and planting connect the various parts of the plan.

Large buildings were surrounded with magnificent parks before the twentieth century. Kings of France glorified themselves at Versailles. The New York International Airport is a twentieth-century recreation of the Versailles plan. Grandeur, once the sole property of kings, is now a part of our great democracy and is symbolic of the splendor of air travel.

International Airport.

Engraved view of Versailles, by J. Rigaud. (Courtesy of the Metropolitan Museum of Art, New York — Dick Fund, 1953)

ARCHITECTURE FOR GOVERNING

Think, for a moment, of the buildings in your community that are connected with governing. No doubt there is a town or city hall, a courthouse, police and fire departments for protection, and a post office, the message center. These structures help people to live together.

If you happen to live in the governing city of your state, there is a large, impressive capitol. As we shall see, the Capitol in Washington is the seat of government for our country as a whole. There the laws that regulate our society are passed.

In former times there were not as many different examples of architecture for governing. The King was governor and ruled from his palace. The PALACE AT VERSAILLES, France, is the most famous palace in the world. From here Louis XIV and his successors, in lavish surroundings, held sway over the lives of their subjects.

53

Wayne Andrews

Versailles.

The monarch insisted that all members of his court live with him rather than in nearby Paris. He hired the architect, Jules Hardouin-Mansart, to expand his little palace into a huge structure to hold ten thousand people — not very comfortably, though, for their living quarters were up under the roof.

They could look out square casement windows onto the backs of statues surmounting the Ionic porticoes of the second floor. There the king lived and entertained. His chambers of state, including the famous "Hall of Mirrors," are among the most sumptuous ever built, with lofty ceilings gilded and painted.

The arched windows admitting light to these rooms could be opened like doors and therefore required railings called "balustrades," to keep people from falling. The first floor contained the quarters of the palace guards as well as utility and storage rooms.

The king commissioned André Lenôtre to plan the gardens, which are as impressive as the palace. Broad avenues lead to reflecting pools, fountains, statues, and summerhouses. Everything is arranged geometrically in rectangles, squares, and circles. Here, under the vast sky, the courtiers and their ladies could enjoy entertainments and walks in the fresh air.

Versailles is architecture for royal governing, a proud building crowned with flaming urns and carved Roman trophies of war, helmets and breastplates, signifying the prowess of the king's armies. The palace and grounds cost over 55 million dollars, for which the people of France were heavily taxed. They finally objected to such extravagance and overthrew the monarchy to establish a government by the people.

54

Independence Hall.

The most important landmark and center for government connected with the founding of the United States is the State House in Philadelphia, which we know as INDEPENDENCE HALL.

Andrew Hamilton, an amateur architect, designed the building. It stands as one of the finest American Renaissance structures in our country.

Hamilton used brick as the principal building material. He accented the doorways, window frames, and tower with white woodwork, as

55

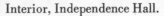

National Park Service photo by Warren A. McCullough

Jefferson did at Monticello. The tower features a superb window of the type known as "Palladian."*

The tower is an unusual feature of Independence Hall in that it was placed outside the building to accommodate the beautifully designed staircase, which otherwise would have taken up valuable interior space. The Liberty Bell is at the foot of the stairs, which lead up past the Palladian window, whose cornice and pilasters are repeated on the inside in the Ionic order.

* Named for Andrea Palladio (1518-1580), Italian architect, whose buildings and books on architecture influenced many English and American architects and builders. The window bearing his name consists of an arch-topped central section ornamented with moldings and keystone block, flanked on either side with upright rectangles. The three units were divided and framed by pilasters with capitals and topped with a horizontal cornice broken in the center by the arch.

Noble, Roman-style Doric columns and a cornice of massive size dignify the main hallway, which leads to the equally stately Declaration Chamber. Here, in 1776, the Declaration of Independence was signed in a setting of elegant informality most fitting for the event and the earnest consultations that went before it.

The architect, in planning his building, changed the palace plan to make it suitable for a democratic form of government. Democracy requires meeting rooms where representatives of the people may congregate — in contrast to palace audience chambers where kings may conduct private conversations.

It can easily be seen that Hamilton not only designed a beautiful building, but also a very practical one. Beyond all else, great architecture serves the purpose for which it is intended. The plan of the building is developed from the use to which it will be put.

Declaration Chamber, Independence Hall.

Three Lions, New York

Capitol, Washington, D. C.

Many chapters make up the story of the building of the CAPITOL in Washington, D.C. Begun by an amateur architect, Dr. William Thornton, whose plans were approved by Washington and Jefferson, the building was continued by Benjamin Latrobe from 1814 to 1817.

Latrobe was the first professionally trained architect to work in this country. He completed the chamber for the House of Representatives, now designated Statuary Hall, and invented two orders of the classical type, one using corn, the other tobacco leaves — two American plants now known around the world.

The next architect to try his hand at completing the great structure was Charles Bulfinch, famous for his State House, in Boston. He succeeded in constructing the central rotunda, which he covered with a shallow dome in the manner of the Pantheon.

From 1855 to 1865, uninterrupted by the Civil War, a fourth architect, Thomas Walter, achieved the present dome, made of cast iron, and designed two great wings to provide more space for the Senate and the House of Representatives (the section to the right in the picture). Even in the 1960's, work on the Capitol continued with the moving out of the East Front to gain more space, and the replacement of crumbling sculpture and stonework.

The architecture of the Capitol began in the Roman style favored by Jefferson. The three-story division of the façades follows palace architecture: a base of heavy stone, a high second floor — the main floor — with pilasters and columns and windows emphasized by pediments, and an attic story with small, square windows.

By the time Walter built his large, many-layered dome, the European Renaissance style of building had gained favor in America.

The Capitol grew with the country, even receiving materials from different states: Virginia sandstone, Massachusetts marble. Rising over the whole structure to unify the various parts created by several different builders is the dome — a symbol of unity and strength which supports a statue of Freedom, guarding her favored land.

Corn Capital, by Latrobe, United States Capitol.

United Nations Building.

Twice in the twentieth century the nations have tried to make world government a reality, first at the League of Nations in Geneva, Switzerland, and then at the UNITED NATIONS in New York. Like the Capitol in Washington, the buildings of the United Nations employed several architects, an international group. Le Corbusier, whose chapel at Ronchamp we have seen, provided a basic design which was somewhat altered as the structures were completed.

The buildings were carefully planned to include office space, conference rooms, a library, a cafeteria, and a restaurant, as well as a very large auditorium for meetings of the General Assembly. A chapel for prayer and meditation was also provided, as well as ample space for thousands of visitors each year.

Construction began in 1949 and ended in 1952. In keeping with the international character of the organization, the materials came from many lands. Britain supplied the limestone for the facing of the Assembly Hall. Italian marble, and rare woods from the Congo, Norway, Canada, the Philippines, and Guatemala enrich the interior.

The tall building, rising serenely like a memorial column, contains the offices of the Secretariat. It is one of the first spectacularly high constructions of aluminum and glass, and is faced at each end with gray Vermont marble.

The Assembly Building is a low, sweeping structure, its curved roof line contrasting with the vertical Secretariat tower. Seven doors lead into the cathedral-like lobby, softly lighted through special glass which appears as veined stone on the exterior. The stairs lead to public galleries where visitors may observe meetings.

The twentieth-century architecture of the United Nations buildings, placed in a finely landscaped setting, is in keeping with the twentieth-century idea of world government and peace: inspiring, therefore almost religious in feeling; daring, therefore dramatic; hopeful, therefore optimistic — a notable example of architecture for governing.

United Nations

Hail, Caesar! by Gérôme.

ARCHITECTURE FOR PLEASURE
AND LEARNING

Several forms of architecture have been invented to provide people with
space to assemble for entertainment. For example, almost every town in
ancient Greece had its open-air theater, usually placed on a hillside into
which the seats were cut to form a semicircle.

The Romans developed this design by putting two theaters together,
using an elaborate system of arches and vaults to create a freestanding
amphitheater, or an "around theater." The seats were arranged in oval
form, pierced only by stairways for the audience to use before and after
the spectacles, which were given in the daytime. An enormous awning
shielded the many spectators from the hot sun. Various contests took
place in the amphitheaters, which were forerunners of the modern sports
stadium.

Colosseum.

The COLOSSEUM is the most famous amphitheater in the world. Here, fifty thousand Romans watched their favorite gladiators, professional fighters, test their strength and skill, sometimes against each other, sometimes against wild animals. During the persecutions by Roman emperors, Christians were put to death here.

Although its story is gloomy, the Colosseum is one of the most magnificent buildings in all the years of architecture. Only a great ghost remains of its once enormous body, for stone upon stone was removed to construct many other later buildings.

John B. Bayley

Roman arched and vaulted construction made possible such a supreme example of the builder's art. Arches like those of the aqueduct bridge at Nîmes, which we have previously seen, curve over and over again in three levels, one on top of another. The fourth story is a wall with small windows and stone hooks for the ropes that supported the awning.

Notice that half columns separate the arches to stop our eyes from following their curves forever and to direct our eyes upward past the solemn Tuscan capitals of the first level, the elegant Ionic of the second, and the rich Corinthian of the third. Many buildings in Europe and America copied this system of orders from the Colosseum.

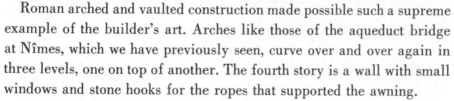

Such perfect balance between curved and straight lines, horizontals and verticals, created a majestic building that seems forever poised, eternal. No wonder an ancient historian wrote, "As long as the Colosseum stands, Rome shall stand; when the Colosseum falls, Rome will fall; when Rome falls, the world will fall."

63

Screen Traveler, from Gendreau, New Yo

Paris Opera House.

Opera is a form of musical drama. The actors are singers, who tell the story by singing rather than speaking their parts. A large orchestra accompanies the singers and occasionally plays by itself. The whole effect of music, beautiful costumes, scenery, and lighting is very grand.

When Charles Garnier built the PARIS OPERA HOUSE, he did not invent a new architecture for his time, the 1860's. Rather he picked and chose from classical Greek and Roman and later Italian and French architecture. He blended things together skillfully so that the Opera House became a masterpiece of its kind.

64

As we have noted in the Colosseum, many arched entrances make it possible for the spectators to assemble quickly just before each performance. Huge groups of sculpture set off the arches at each end of the long façade to indicate the main entrances. Even larger sculptures ornament the roof. In between, on the second floor is an enormous reception hall reached by the famous stairway, which also leads to the upper balconies of the auditorium where the operas take place.

More sculpture and colored marbles enrich the interior with its many curved lines. Balconies curve outward and, during the intermissions, ladies can see and be seen in their fine clothes. Notice that the steps curve outward at the bottom of each flight, but curve inward at the top. The architect was very careful to work out every part of his building so that all the parts together would create a luxurious setting.

Stairway, Paris Opera House.

Eiffel Tower.

The EIFFEL TOWER was built for the World's Fair in Paris, 1889. Everyone enjoys going to fairs, and architects welcome an opportunity to design exposition buildings because they can experiment with new ideas.

Gustave Eiffel, an engineer, selected wrought iron as the material for his structure because he could calculate exactly how thick and how long each piece should be in order to do its part in supporting and steadying the entire framework. Metal has this advantage over other materials: its performance as part of a building can be accurately predicted.

Eiffel constructed the skeleton for a building. Its purpose as an observation tower and as an engineering exhibition piece did not require enclosure with glass or other materials. It proved that a structure 984 feet high, weighing seven thousand tons, resting on stone and concrete mats in the ground, could be successfully erected. It actually pointed the way to the skyscraper and modern construction.

Travel and Transport Building.

The Chicago Century of Progress Exposition in 1933 startled and pleased Americans with its brightly colored new architecture. Since then, what we call contemporary architecture — architecture that is of our time and does not imitate previous buildings — has met with increasing success.

The architects who designed the TRAVEL AND TRANSPORT BUILDING used the principles of suspension bridges like the Brooklyn and Golden Gate bridges in New York and San Francisco.

The roof was a dome made of metal plates suspended from steel cables. These cables were attached to twelve steel towers, steadied by other cables which were firmly anchored by huge slabs of concrete. The

Kaufmann-Fabry, Chicago

roof plates overlapped so that they could slide over each other as temperature changes, winds, and loads of rain or snow caused differences of as much as six feet in the size of the dome. It was approximately 200 feet across, covering more space than the domes of St. Peter's or the Capitol in Washington.

Such a building was frankly experimental and was therefore important, because experiments lead to discoveries. And discoveries, in turn, lead to improvements in architecture, as they do in every other human activity.

67

The Solomon R. Guggenheim Museum

We can gain both pleasure and learning from museums, libraries, schools, and colleges. Architects from ancient to modern times have designed all types of educational institutions. One of the most unusual buildings of this kind is the GUGGENHEIM MUSEUM, created by the American architect, Frank Lloyd Wright.

When Wright was a young man he worked with Louis Sullivan, whom he later called his "master." Both men helped to free architecture from

the past and invented new forms. They were also writers, almost preachers, for their architectural faith, which decreed that the form of the building must take its shape from the purpose or function that the building is to serve. Wright chose to build his museum as a spiraling ramp down which visitors walk, viewing the pictures as they go. The core of the spiral is a great circular space covered by a glass dome.

Wright was first admired abroad, especially in Japan where he built a hotel that withstood earthquake shocks. In the United States he created several houses and office buildings using materials in harmony with their locations. As far back as the early 1900's he made concrete respectable. Up until then it was a material thought appropriate only for useful structures such as factories and garages.

Concrete can be shaped in any form that will hold it firmly until it becomes hard. Because curved forms are expensive to build, Wright developed square forms, often with angled sides. In his museum he used both curved and square forms, thereby achieving shapes that contrast with each other.

You will notice that the large shapes are strongly horizontal. The building appears to press upon the earth, to be almost a part of it. It was a favorite idea of this architect that his structures were as one with nature.

The Solomon R. Guggenheim Museum

Procession in St. Mark's Square, from a painting by Gentile Bellini in the Accademia, Venice.

A WALK AROUND ST. MARK'S SQUARE

This book began with a picture of an imaginary square in an imaginary city — an exercise in perspective and architectural drawing. This book ends with a walking tour of the most famous square in the world, ST. MARK'S in Venice, a very real square in a seemingly unreal city built many centuries ago over the waters of the Adriatic Sea.

We shall find, as we saw in the first picture, a grouping of buildings raised for different human needs. Let us begin by going through a doorway at one end of the square. We have also stepped back in time — to the year 1496 — and are attending a religious ceremony, the Corpus Christi Day procession of the Relics of Christ's Cross, carried in an elaborate box on the shoulders of four men.

70

The choir goes first. Candle bearers follow, as well as members of a religious brotherhood. On the far right, more than halfway down the square, walking beneath a golden umbrella, is the Doge of Venice, the ruler of the city.

Facing us is ST. MARK'S BASILICA, begun in 830 A.D. as a chapel for the PALACE OF THE DOGES, which is to the right. Golden pictures above the doors of the Basilica glitter brilliantly in the sunlight as it reflects from the thousands of tiny bits of glass mosaic of which the pictures are made.

Three hundred years after this event, the square had changed only a little, as you will see in the next picture.

View of St. Mark's Square, by Canaletto. (Grenville L. Winthrop Bequest, Fogg Art Museum, Harvard University, Cambridge, Mass.)

Think of this square as a room. (It has been called the ballroom of Europe.) The pavement is the floor. The buildings left, right, and at the rear, are the walls. We can imagine the sky as a great dome, the ceiling. We sense the space within the room because we can see where it stops. We can also appreciate or feel space by moving through it, by changing our position in relation to the different parts of the room.

This imaginary walk around the square is planned to give you, as best we can from pictures on a flat page, the impression of moving through architecturally created space, the unique element of architecture that the other arts do not possess.

Architects can tell us by various means how large or how small are the spaces they create. Sometimes they can trick us into believing that

72

spaces are larger than they actually are. For example, the two bands of white designs on the pavement carry our eyes across the square to the Basilica, which would seem nearer if the pavement was plain. Place your fingers over the bands and you will see that the church seems to move slightly forward.

Walking down the right-hand band, with the famous pigeons of the square scurrying from under our feet, we stop halfway before the domed and arched, carved and colored jewel box that is St. Mark's. We stop because our way is barred momentarily by three very tall flagpoles from which once flew the flags of Cyprus, Crete, and Morea, three eastern colonies of Venice when she was Queen of the Seas and the wealth of East and West passed through her hands.

The flagpoles mark the space immediately in front of the church — space that flows into the portals, through the turrets, and around the domes. The poles create a feeling of spaciousness that we might miss if they were taken away.

Philip Gendreau, New York

Interior, St. Mark's.

Leaving the world of man for a moment, we enter the world of the spirit, the most sumptuous Byzantine church that has lasted the years since it was built. Richly veined marbles sheathe its lower walls; its upper vaults and pendentives covered with mosaics represent angels and saints — St. Mark himself, writer of one of the four Gospels of the Bible, and patron saint of Venice.

But these are details that divert our eyes. As in Hagia Sophia, which St. Mark's resembles, the architect created exalting interior space with four great arches, enclosing it. A windowed dome caps it. Beyond there is another dome sheltering the altar, with a curving apse behind. The thick walls, pierced with repeating arches, hold in the space which seems to be pushing on the vaults and domes above.

74

On our way in and out of the church we passed through the portals of the façade, built in the early Middle Ages. Columns support columns, from which arches spring to create shadowed space. Sunlight falls across the many-colored marbles of the stonework in lively contrast to the shadows.

On rainy days, waterspouts, just below the railing, carry off water from the roof where today the four famous bronze horses of St. Mark's gleam, faintly golden. Once they were gilded, and drew a chariot atop a triumphal arch in Rome. They were carried away to Istanbul and finally back again to Italy — to Venice.

The horses look proudly across to the winged lion, the companion of St. Mark, on the CLOCK TOWER, which was built at the end of the Middle Ages. A banner, advertising an exhibition, hangs in the arch at pavement level. In a few minutes the two bronze men on top of the tower will strike the big bell to tell us it is noon and time for lunch.

Clock Tower, St. Mark's Square.

Philip Gendreau, New York

The Square and the Little Square of St. Mark's, by Canaletto. (Courtesy Wadsworth Athenaeum, Hartford, Conn.)

If we walk toward the Clock Tower and turn our backs to it, this is the view we see. The square is to the right, with the shops below and offices above in the so-called "NEW OFFICES," built in 1640. To the left is the LITTLE SQUARE, a narrow space leading down to the water beyond the columns in the distance.

Between the two, where the large square turns into the smaller, is the soaring BELL TOWER. This high structure is a kind of obelisk, marking the location of the entire group of buildings that form the two squares. Originally it was made of wood and served as a signpost and lighthouse for ships at sea. In 1329 the tower was rebuilt in brick, and another lion of St. Mark was placed to decorate its top. By 1902 the tower was so weakened by age that one day it quietly fell into a pile of dust. The accident hurt no one and damaged only the LOGGETTA, the little building at the tower's base. Both buildings were restored.

The Loggetta was the office for the Commander of the Guard during meetings of the Grand Council, the governing body of the city. It was ornamented with statues and reliefs by the architect-sculptor, Sansovino, who also designed the LIBRARY, which forms one side of the Little Square.

Sansovino left Florence, where he was born, and went to Rome. There he learned Renaissance building based on old Roman structures. When he arrived in Venice he found that the Venetians were fond of luxury and display. He therefore enriched his designs to please them, using much sculpture and placing statues on the roofs, to make the tops of his buildings more interesting.

The Library is his best-known building. Its front consists of two arched colonnades, one on top of the other, lavishly decorated with sculpture which includes a richly carved frieze of garlands, masks, and children just below the top railing. Light and shadow flicker over the façade. Space flows into the many arches of the very long building. Turn to page 43 to see again the picture, painted in Florence, that Sansovino may have had in mind when he planned his masterpiece, the Library.

Library, St. Mark's Square.

The Little Square in Venice, by Canaletto. (National Gallery of Art, Washington, D.C. — Samuel H. Kress Collection)

The PALACE OF THE DOGES, rebuilt in the late Middle Ages just before Bellini painted his procession picture (pages 70-71), forms the other side of the Little Square, opposite Sansovino's Library. The building is remarkable for its very deep colonnades with pointed arches. The lowest ones extend the space from the square into the building, and give the impression that the structure is floating on posts — lifted off the ground, not unlike a modern skyscraper.

Space also flows through the intricate stonework of the second-floor colonnade, which can be entered from within the palace. The third-floor walls are made of pink and white stone, arranged in geometric patterns and broken by a few large windows, one of which features a balcony and sculpture. A spiky parapet edges the roof.

The building suggests that perhaps a Venetian trader found it in the

East and had it floated over the sea to Venice, where it set the style for many other smaller palaces throughout the city.

We finish our tour of the square with space itself, which closes the Little Square. The pavement ends and water begins where gondolas, the taxi-boats of Venice, await their customers. The looming Palace of the Doges looks down in regal manner upon the time-stained Library.

Two gigantic columns brought from Syria rise against the wall of space. The right-hand one bears St. Theodore, an early patron saint of Venice, with his crocodile; the left-hand shaft supports the symbol of the city, the Lion of St. Mark.

Alinari, Florence

TIME CHART OF HISTORICAL PERIODS
(Based on periods of 500 years)

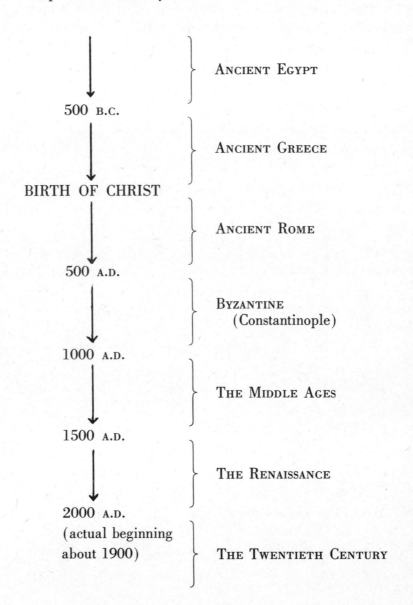

500 B.C. — ANCIENT EGYPT

ANCIENT GREECE

BIRTH OF CHRIST

ANCIENT ROME

500 A.D.

BYZANTINE
(Constantinople)

1000 A.D.

THE MIDDLE AGES

1500 A.D.

THE RENAISSANCE

2000 A.D.
(actual beginning
about 1900)

THE TWENTIETH CENTURY

SOME ARCHITECTURAL TERMS

ABUTMENT — a part of a wall built to receive pressure, such as that of an arch

AMPHITHEATER — an oval or circular building with rising rows of seats around an open space

APSE — the eastern or altar end of a church, usually in the form of a half-circle and roofed with a half-dome or vaulting

ARCH — a curving structure made of wedge-shaped parts, used to span an opening, and capable of supporting weight from above

BALUSTRADE — a row of short, ornamental columns topped by a rail

BUTTRESS — a structure built out against a wall or building to give support and strength

CASEMENT — a window sash opening on hinges, like a door

CLAPBOARDS — overlapping boards to seal out moisture, wind, etc.

COLONNADES — rows of columns connected at their tops by a cornice, sometimes roofed

COLUMN — a pillar supporting a roof; for a further discussion of types of columns, see page 12

CORNICE — the horizontal molded projection at the top of a building

DOME — a large roof shaped like half a sphere; for more about domes, see page 13

FACADE — the front of a building

FLECHE — a tall, thin spire, so named from the French word for arrow

FLUTING — a decoration of parallel grooves

GARGOYLE — a waterspout, often grotesquely carved, jutting from the eaves of a building

LINTEL — a horizontal piece across the top of an opening, often placed to carry the weight of the structure above it

MINARETS — towers often built on Moslem churches (mosques) from which the faithful are called to prayer

MOSAIC — a flat decoration made by setting small pieces of glass or stone of different colors into some other material, to form a design or picture

NAVE — the central or main body of a church, running lengthwise from the main entrance

OBELISK — a four-sided pillar that tapers toward the top and ends in a pyramid

PARAPETS — low walls about the edge of a roof, terrace, bridge, or fort

PEDIMENT — originally the triangular space that forms the gable of a roof; now any low, triangular decoration resembling a gable — possibly above a door

PENDENTIVE — one of the triangular pieces at the corners of a rectangular or square room to support a circular roof or dome

PERISTYLE — an arrangement of roof-supporting columns

PIER — a mass of masonry used to strengthen a wall

PILASTER — an upright column built into a wall and projecting slightly from it

PORTICO — a row of columns supporting a roof, around or at the entrance of a building

RAFTER — one of the sloping timbers that supports a roof

RAMP — a sloping passage without steps, connecting different levels

ROTUNDA — a round building, especially one with a dome

SCAFFOLDS — temporary elevated platforms for support of workmen and materials

THATCH — a roof covering, often of straw, to shed water

VAULT — an arched structure, usually forming a ceiling or roof; for an explanation of *barrel vault*, see page 13

82